IMAGES
of America

MAPLEWOOD

Charlotte Iona Crowell (1881–1957) wore this dress when she graduated from the high school of the township of South Orange in the Columbia School Hall (the predecessor of Columbia High School) on Thursday evening, June 21, 1900. She had the foresight to save photographs and records assembled by her uncle, Horace Crowell, add to the collection, and pass it on to her grandson, John Crowell Bausmith, and her neighbor, Howard Willard Wiseman. With fond memories, we dedicate this book to "Grandma Salter" (Mrs. Charlotte Iona Crowell Salter).

—John C. Bausmith and Howard W. Wiseman

IMAGES
of America

MAPLEWOOD

Durand-Hedden
House and Garden Association

ARCADIA
PUBLISHING

Published by Arcadia Publishing
Charleston, South Carolina

Library of Congress Catalog Card Number: 2008927306

For all general information contact Arcadia Publishing at:
Telephone 843-853-2070
Fax 843-853-0044
E-mail sales@arcadiapublishing.com
For customer service and orders:
Toll-Free 1-888-313-2665

Visit us on the Internet at www.arcadiapublishing.com

Maplewood's first automobile was a 1907 White Model G steam touring car made by the White Sewing Machine Company of Cleveland, Ohio. Clarence B. Riker is at the steering wheel with his son, Carleton B. Riker Sr., next to him. In the rear seat are Jessie Carpenter Riker (right, the wife of the driver), and her two sisters. The photograph was taken in the driveway of what is now 25 Mountain Avenue. (Courtesy of Carleton B. Riker Jr. and Andrew H. Bobeck.)

CONTENTS

ACKNOWLEDGMENTS

The authors express their appreciation to the following organizations and individuals for making this book possible: the Columbia High School Library, Joseph Fanning, librarian; the Durand-Hedden House and Garden Association, Jean Evans*, president; the Immaculate Heart of Mary Church; *Maplewood Matters* magazine, Karen Duncan, editor; the Maplewood Memorial Library, Rowland Bennett, director; the Morrow Memorial United Methodist Church; *News-Record of Maplewood and South Orange*, Mark Hrywna, managing editor; the Prospect Presbyterian Church; St. Joseph's Catholic Church; the Seth Boyden School; Sickles Photo-Reporting Service, Peter Sickles; The Strollers, Judi Gajary; the Township of Maplewood, Ellen Davenport and Roger Desiderio; The Woman's Club of Maplewood; Louise Noll; Mary Auth; Jeanne L. Bausmith; Charles Bibbins; Andrew H. Bobeck; Art Christensen; Jay Gavitt, subject chair of social studies K-12 for the South Orange-Maplewood School System; Robert H. Grasmere; Gertrude Haas; Lee Horner; Janet Koch; Althea MacWhorter; Susan Newberry; Henry E. Niemitz; Joseph Veach Noble; John Overall; Carleton B. Riker Jr.; Peter B. Sickley; Robert C. Sickley Jr.; Alan Siegel; Joan Lowell Smith; Mildred Staley; Joyce Stibitz; Henry T. Wallhauser; Audree S. Weil; Marilyn White; Ann Wilson; and Norman Woolley.

*Jean Evans (1924–1998), wife of John R. Evans Jr., M.D., was an active president of the Durand-Hedden House and Garden Association until the day she died on May 28, 1998. Jean, dressed in her period costume, was a very energetic, caring person, who loved to teach the young people how to churn butter and bake bread in the historic kitchen.

Over the years, she was also extremely active in gardening and garden clubs, the Maplewood Service League, and the high school PTA. She served twice as president of the Columbia Home & School Association and was involved with the stadium food stands, the scholarship fund, and the floral decorations at graduation. She was a past president of the Maplewood Garden Club, past president of the Garden Club of New Jersey, and a member of the New Jersey Chrysanthemum Society.

Jean's leadership and support as president of Durand-Hedden inspired us to proceed with the publication of this book on Maplewood. She enjoyed living life to the fullest and will be greatly missed.

—John C. Bausmith and Howard W. Wiseman

INTRODUCTION

The name Maplewood dates back to 1860, when a name for the first railroad station was needed. The town's history, however, can be traced back many more years to a time when the first settlers purchased land from the Lenni-Lenape Indians. When the settlers, primarily of English descent, traveled to New Jersey from Connecticut, they landed in Newark in 1666. The settlers came in contact with Lenni-Lenape Indian chiefs, who sold them a vast track of land bounded by the Passaic River on one side and mountains to the west on the other side. Most of the early settlers stayed near the river and founded the city of Newark. Others began to move west, and by the early 1700s, farms or plantations were established at the foothills of the mountains. One of these settlements was located in the western half of what is now Maplewood. It had no name until the late eighteenth century, when it was called Jefferson Village after Thomas Jefferson. It really was the most northern section of Springfield Township.

The eastern, or Hilton, section, originally called North Farms or Middleville, developed after the opening of the Newark-Springfield Turnpike (now Springfield Avenue) in 1806. In 1880, with the granting of a post office to the area, the name Hilton was adopted. There already was another Middleville with a post office in New Jersey.

Jefferson Village and Middleville officially came together in 1863, when South Orange Township annexed Jefferson Village from Millburn Township. Thus, we find it convenient to present this volume in eleven chapters illustrating the main phases of life in both sections of the Township of Maplewood at the same time, rather than explaining the histories of the two areas separately.

Famous people lived in both sections of Maplewood. Seth Boyden (1788–1870) settled in Hilton in 1855 after starting several successful industries in Newark as a result of his inventions. He made the first malleable iron, the first two steam engines for the Morris & Essex Railroad, daguerreotypes (photographs), and patent leather. While here, Boyden cultivated the huge "Hilton Strawberries," which brought prosperity to the Hilton farmers. The Seth Boyden Elementary School and Boyden Avenue were named after him.

In the section that became Jefferson Village dwelled Timothy Ball, a cousin of George Washington. During the Revolutionary War, General George Washington visited the Ball Homestead on Ridgewood Road several times. The Timothy Ball House once served as a restaurant called the Washington Inn and is now a private home.

As a boy, our 26th president, Theodore Roosevelt, spent summer months at the 100-acre estate of his aunt and uncle, Laura and Cornelius Van Schaick Roosevelt. They had no children of their own. In his youth, Theodore Roosevelt was frail and suffered from asthma, so he was sent from his home in New York City to "The Hickories" in Maplewood to enjoy nature and the clear mountain air.

A famous native son was Asher Brown Durand (1796–1886), who lived on the corner of Ridgewood and Durand Roads. Durand became a world-famous engraver and painter in the 19th century. He was a founder of the Hudson River school of landscape painting, and his masterpieces are in the art collections of major museums and other prominent locations in this country.

The development of the railroad, with its convenience to Newark and New York City, changed this area from a farming community to a suburban town. People from all over the country, who acquired jobs in the cities, came here by the thousands during the early part of the 20th century so they could easily commute to work by mass transit and leave their cars at home for their families. The excellent schools and beautiful surroundings were also a big attraction. To this day, many second and third generations have remained here to enjoy the rural atmosphere, but still have the convenience of easy access to the busy cities.

We hope this volume will bring back memories for some people, and for others, provide knowledge of the history of Maplewood that has made it such a special place to live over the years.

This painting of Asher B. Durand's birthplace by Elias W. Durand shows the farmhouse, which was located on the southwest corner of Ridgewood and Durand Road, with the farm across the street. The Durand-Hedden House, which is still standing, is down the road near the center of the painting.

One

COMMUNITY DEVELOPMENT

JEFFERSON VILLAGE, 1815

This map was engraved by Cyrus Durand in 1815 to support an application to the federal government for a post office for the 30 families in residence in Jefferson Village (now Maplewood). The application was unsuccessful. Maplewood did not attain its own independent post office until 132 years later.

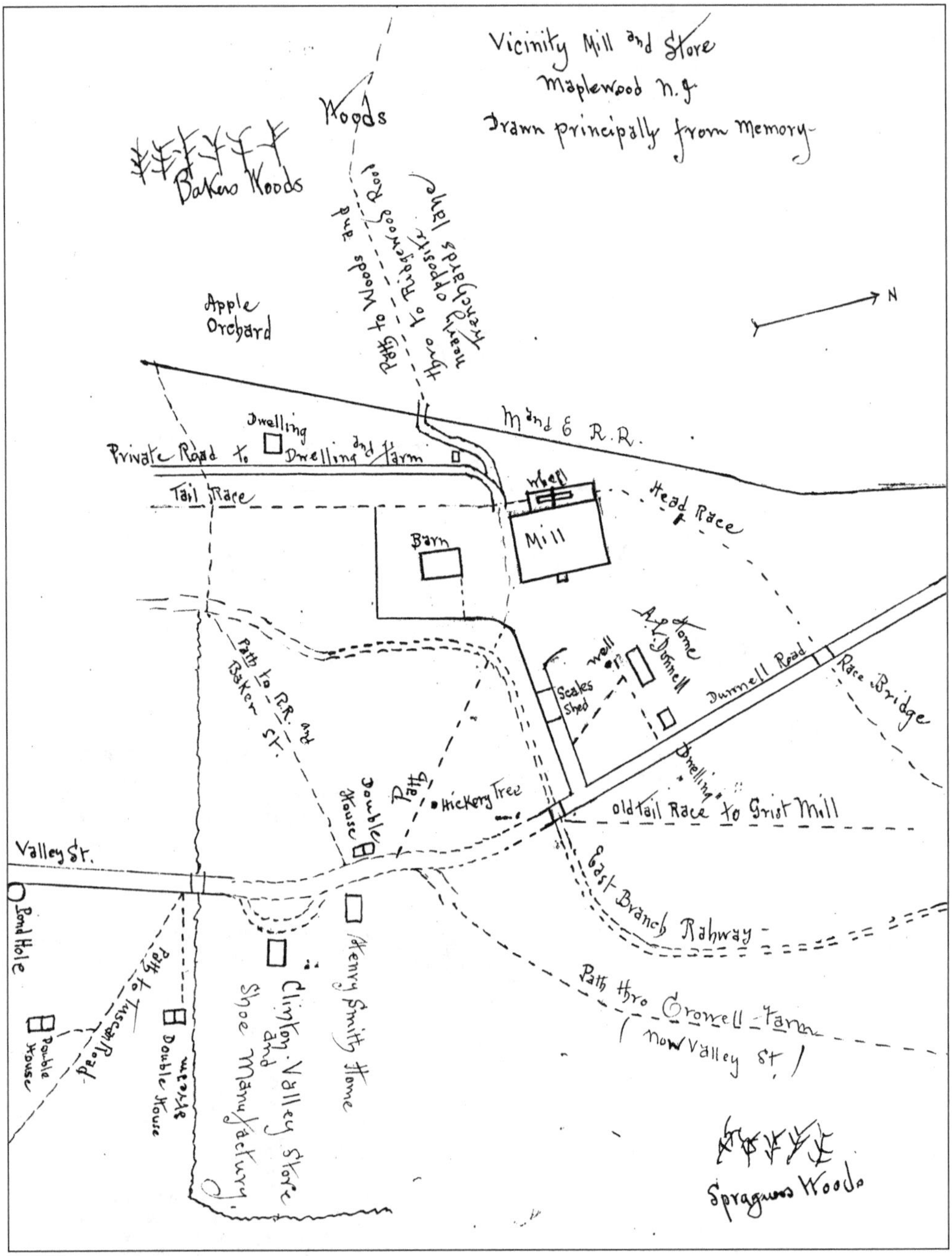
Vicinity Mill and Store
Maplewood N.J.
Drawn principally from Memory
Woods
Bakers Woods
Apple Orchard
Path to Woods and
thro to Ridgewood Road
nearly opposite
Merchards lane
N
M and E R.R.
Dwelling
Private Road to Dwelling and Farm
Tail Race
Wheel
Mill
Head Race
Barn
Well
Scales Shed
A. G. Durnell
Home
Durnell Road
Race Bridge
Path to R.R. and Baker St.
Path
Hickory Tree
Double House
Dwelling
old Tail Race to Grist Mill
Valley St.
East Branch Rahway
Pond Hole
Double House
Path to Tuscan Road
Double House
Clinton Valley Store and Shoe Manufactury
Henry Smith Home
Path thro Crowell Farm
(now Valley St.)
Spragues Woods

This manuscript map, entitled "Vicinity Mill and Store Maplewood, N.J., Drawn principally from Memory," was taken from a notebook by Horace Edwin Crowell (1851–1923), uncle of Charlotte Iona Crowell Salter (see p. 2).

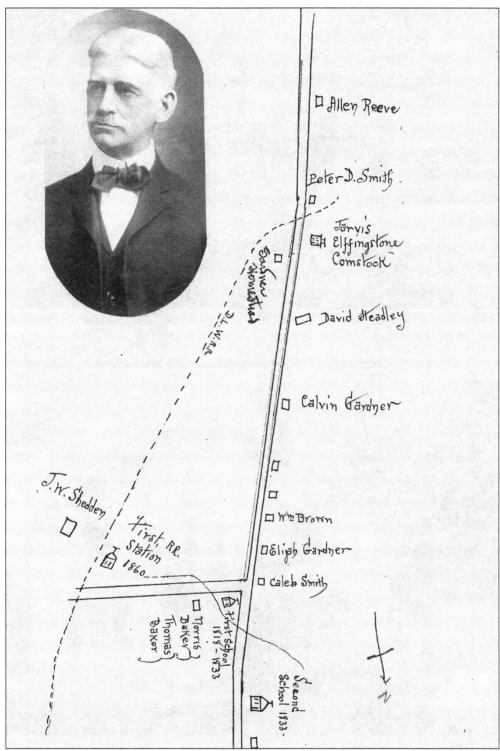

This manuscript map shows Ridgewood Road looking south from the vicinity of Baker Street, indicating dwellings and most of the owners before 1900. (Horace E. Crowell, cartographer.)

"The Hickories" was the home of Mr. and Mrs. Cornelius Van Schaick Roosevelt, aunt and uncle of future president Theodore Roosevelt. The house was erected in 1865 on 100 acres of land that had formerly been the farm of Capt. Isaac Smith. As a boy, Theodore Roosevelt spent many summer months here enjoying the outdoors and recording his observations of nature.

The carriage house, including a horse stable and hayloft for the Roosevelt Estate, was built c. 1865. This building still stands at 104 Durand Road with one side facing Durand Road and the front pointed toward Ridgewood Road.

The summer cottage for the Roosevelt Estate gardener was built *c*. 1870. The remodeled and enlarged house is now the home of Ellen Davenport, former mayor of Maplewood, and her husband, Donald. The house stands at 106 Durand Road.

This house on the Roosevelt Estate was the home of the superintendent of the estate. It stands at a considerable distance from the main house and is now 589 Ridgewood Road at the corner of Curtiss Place. The second schoolhouse in Jefferson Village, which was near the entrance gate of "The Hickories," was abandoned as a school in 1868. The Roosevelts purchased the building and relocated it to the back of this house.

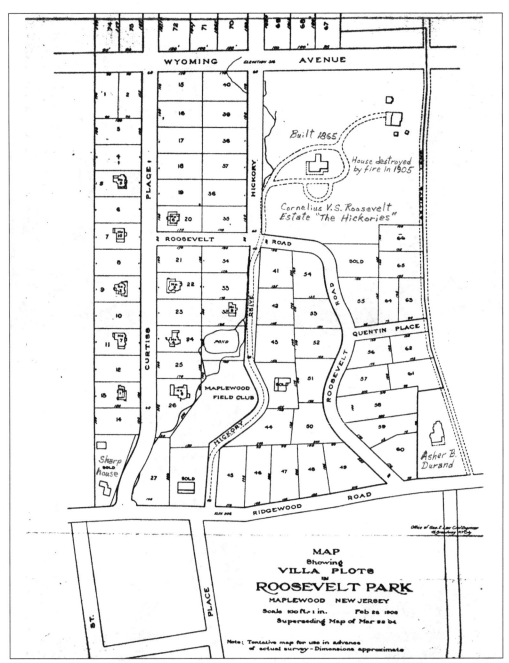

This map shows the layout for Villa Plots in Roosevelt Park in 1905. William H. Curtiss purchased the Roosevelt Estate in 1902 after the death of Mrs. C.V.S. Roosevelt in 1900 in New York City. Notations have been added to indicate the locations of buildings on the Roosevelt property and Asher B. Durand's house on the corner of Ridgewood Road and Artist's Lane, which is now Durand Road. The Sharp House shown on the map was the superintendent's house. The carriage house and gardener's cottage are located near Wyoming Avenue and Artist's Lane. Hickory Drive, with its surviving main gates, was the entrance road to the estate. Quentin was the name of Teddy Roosevelt's youngest son.

14

This house was built in 1869 for Asher Brown Durand (1796–1886), a nationally famous engraver and painter. Asher was born at this site and inherited the property. At the age of 73, he moved back to his birthplace to get away from the noisy city of New York, where he had lived much of his very successful career. The four front windows facing southeast on the third floor provided lots of daylight for his new studio.

This is Asher B. Durand's art studio on the third floor of his home in Maplewood. The small paintings lining the walls are study paintings made directly from nature. He used them to paint some of his large masterpieces, which are in the art collections of major art museums and other prominent locations in this country.

This panoramic view shows the valley in Maplewood with the mountain in the background as it appeared *c.* 1900. At the peak of the mountain to the far left is Washington Rock, where General George Washington was able to view the British troops coming from Staten Island during the Revolutionary War. To the right above Ridgewood Road one can still see some of the surviving farmland.

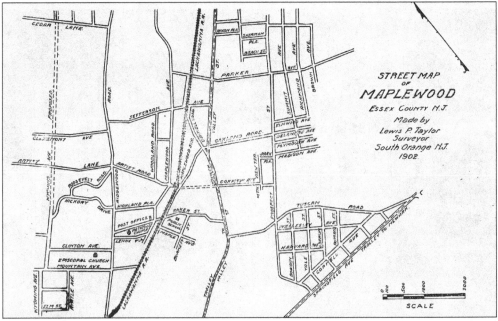

This street map shows Maplewood in 1902 at the turn of the century. One can see a railroad and a trolley line passing through the center of town, providing public transportation into the cities of Newark and New York. Streets have been laid out replacing some of the early farms. Two churches and a public school are also evident.

16

The train on this postcard is headed for a new development being promoted as Model Park in 1910. It was advertised as the "garden spot of Essex County, a veritable Home-seekers' Paradise, the most conveniently located tract imaginable." The advertisement continued by stating that the railroad ran along the western boundary, and the monthly commutation fare was $6.90.

The trolley car shown here is also headed for Model Park in 1910. A promotional booklet, published by H.S. Wyllie in 1911, says, "Three trolley lines have their terminals at the entrance to the Park on Millburn and Roland [now Cypress Street] Avenues, 30-minute trip to Broad and Market Streets, Newark, for 5 cents."

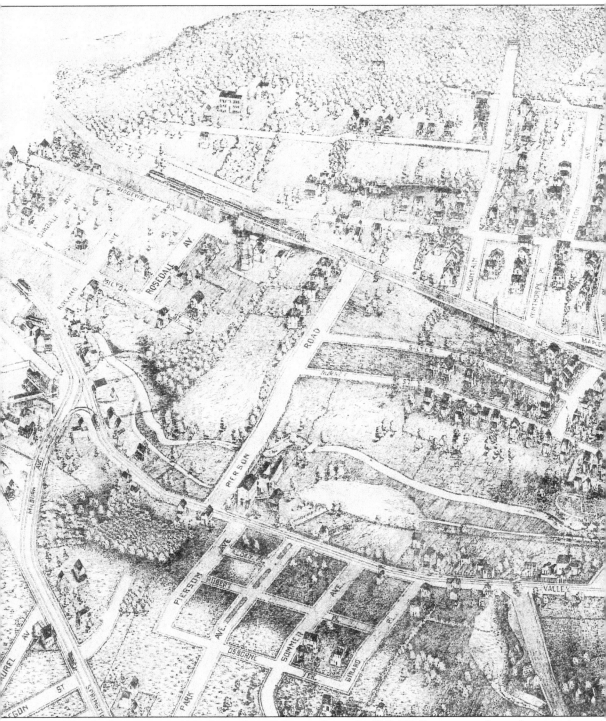

This bird's-eye view of Maplewood in 1910 was drawn by H.S. Wyllie as part of a real estate promotional booklet entitled *Picturesque Maplewood*, published by Wyllie in Newark, New Jersey, in 1911. Proposed developments at that time included Model Park, Vauxhall Terrace, Blue Ridge Park, Valley View, Mountain View Terrace, South Orange Heights, and Hiltonia.

18

One can clearly see the trolley tracks running through the center of town. The east branch of the Rahway River can be seen running through the lowest elevation in the valley, along with the raceway feeding Pierson's Mill pond, which supplied waterpower for the mill.

Based on the buildings shown, the aerial view above was probably photographed in 1921. The railroad can be clearly seen running through the center of town. Housing developments were fast replacing the open farmland. In the next year, the current Maplewood Country Club would replace the Field Club building on Baker Street. The police station, fire headquarters, and the

town hall were still located on Maplewood Avenue in the center. It would be another ten years before the present town hall was constructed. Note that the houses on Baker Street across from Ricalton School have not yet been moved for Memorial Park. There are very few houses above Wyoming Avenue.

The autogyro *Silverbrook* was used to take the 1932 aerial view shown below. Notice the non-retractable landing gear and the open cockpit.

This 1932 aerial, taken by the *Silverbrook* autogyro, shows the town fully developed, except for the areas set aside for the well-planned park system. Springfield Avenue can be clearly seen as a straight diagonal line transversing the photograph, reflecting its origin as an early turnpike (toll road) connecting Newark and Springfield.

Two

HOMES

This is a nineteenth-century view of Valley Street where it intersects Parker Avenue. The Beach Homestead, dating back to 1747, is the smaller house on the left. The Crowell Homestead, on the right, is the second house built at this location by the Crowell family, who originally settled here in 1728. The north end of the house (shown here) was built in 1799, and the south end addition was built in 1835.

The Arcularius House once stood in the triangle made by Tuscan Road and Springfield Avenue. It was built before the American Revolution and was used as a hospital during the Battle of Springfield in 1780.

The Old Stone House (now 22 Jefferson Avenue), built in the mid-18th century, served as a flag stop location for the Morris and Essex Railroad from 1838 to 1860. During this time, it was owned by Daniel Beach and his wife, Betsy Durand Beach, a sister of Asher B. Durand. The kitchen was used as a waiting room during inclement weather until 1860, when the first depot was built near Baker Street on Maplewood Avenue.

The Timothy and Esther Ball House, built in 1743 on Ridgewood Road in Washington Park, is shown as it appeared around 1900. Probably this is close to what it looked like during the Revolutionary War. General George Washington visited here during the war and slept in a room over the kitchen.

The Timothy Ball House was remodeled in the second decade of the 20th century by the Washington Park Company. The small upper window in the stone part of the house is in the room where General Washington slept. This room was kept warm by heat from the large chimney nearby.

The Gardner House, built by Samuel Gardner *c.* 1785, still stands today at 658 Ridgewood Road. It has been converted into a law office and can be easily seen when approaching Maplewood from the Wyoming section of Millburn. The house was passed to Miss Helena Stone from the Gardner family. When she died, the spinning wheel from this house went to the Durand-Hedden House, where it is on display to the public.

The Ezekial Ball Homestead, which still stands at 250 Elmwood Avenue, has characteristics indicating it could have been built as early as 1696 or 1700. It was probably owned by Ezekial Ball in 1750. His father, Thomas Ball, settled in the Maplecrest Park area in 1718. Ezekial was Timothy Ball's brother.

The Hand House, located on the south corner of Valley Street and Tuscan Road, may have been built as early as 1730. Records indicate that William Hand sold part of his farm to Samuel Pierson in 1762. There is a legend that Chief Tuscan had a Native-American encampment on the bank of the stream behind the house, and he was buried there with his horse.

The Aaron Brown Homestead is shown here as it appeared in 1906. It was built in 1805 by Aaron Brown and his wife, Dorcas Ball, on 60 acres of farmland owned by her father. The house still stands at 81 Parker Avenue on the corner of Richmond Avenue.

This painting is a view of the Courter Farm looking west toward the center of Maplewood in the mid- to late 1800s. The farm is located on Tuscan Road above Prospect Street. The area known as Tuscan Hill was used by the Essex County Militia for Muster Days as early as 1794. David B. Courter was still farming here in 1904.

This is a 19th-century photograph of the William Courter Homestead, which is in the painting at the top of the page. The house, with a front addition and roof perpendicular to the old roof, still stands at 91 Tuscan Road.

Looking east at the Courter Farm at the turn of the century, one can see the tall willow trees that once bordered Tuscan Road above Prospect Street. The great fields pastured many cows, and large wagonloads of milk left for Newark daily.

The stone portion of this early house on the Courter Farm is believed to have been built by Jonas Ball around 1750 as a cooper's shop for making barrels. An adjacent spring would have supplied plenty of water required for soaking the wood. The basement of the house was used by the Courters as a cool storage facility for milk from their extensive dairy farm. The house, sometimes referred to as the "Spring House," still stands today at 88 Tuscan Road.

This is a view of Pierson's Pond with the house in the background. In 1831, Lewis Pierson built a 300-foot dam flooding 15 acres of land, which provided the source of waterpower to operate the mill until 1909. In the winter, the millpond was also a popular spot for ice skating. The area is now part of the Maplewood Country Club golf course.

Lewis Pierson built the mill in 1831, and this Greek Revival house in 1843 (it is shown here in 1906). The Pierson property consisted of 250 acres of land purchased in the 1760s from the heirs of some of the original plantation owners. The business today is still being operated by the Pierson family.

This picture of the Philander Ball House was taken in 1897. The members of the Ball family shown here, from left to right, are John, Anna, Philander, Warren, and Lizzie. The house was built in 1849 and still stands at 172 Parker Avenue.

Seth Boyden lived in this house from 1855 until 1870. The school named after him can be seen in the background (see p. 60 for more on Seth Boyden).

This photograph is a view looking up the mountain from the bottom of what is now Ridgewood Terrace before the street was put through. It was taken from a point on Ridgewood Road in front of where the Morrow Memorial United Methodist Church stands today.

This is the same view after Ridgewood Terrace was put through and Mr. Edward C. Balch had erected 41 houses on it. In total, Mr. Balch built 175 houses in Maplewood on the west side of the railroad tracks.

This view of the mid-19th-century Fleming House was photographed in the late 1800s from Boyden Avenue. Even though the house still faces Boyden Avenue, the entrance today is 304 Elmwood Avenue. It has 12-foot-high ceilings, marble fireplaces, and much of the original furnishings, including oil paintings by a member of the Fleming family.

The Marcus L. Ward Home looked like this when it was built in 1927 on 49 acres bounded by Boyden, Springfield, and Elmwood Avenues. Shown here is a view of the outside of the east wing of the dormitory and the lounge. The Ward Homestead was initially opened as a free home for 80 bachelors and widowers over 60 years old who could no longer support themselves.

Danny Morrison lived in this house at 15 Highland Place for more than 50 years. He had many jobs in town during the second half of the 19th century, including being a trustee and janitor of the Jefferson Village School, but he is best remembered for being the town lamp lighter. He jogged about town in his horse and buggy at dusk, stopping to light the streetlights.

The Van Iderstine family owned this home for many years before it had to be torn down to make way for the construction of the present Maplewood Municipal Building on Valley Street.

Hezekiah Dare built this house on Valley Street near Oakview Avenue in 1840; according to the present owner, nothing on the inside or outside has really changed. Emory H. Dare, a grandson of Hezekiah, was the tax collector for the Township of Maplewood from 1948 until 1963, the year he died. The house is now 592 Valley Street.

This house, which no longer exists, was the Valley Street home of Professor James Ricalton from 1871 until 1924. Ricalton was hired as Maplewood's first permanent schoolmaster in 1871. He traveled to remote parts of the world during school vacations and became a famous photographer. The large addition on the right (south) side of the original house was built to house Ricalton's collection of curios gathered from his travels (see p. 61 for more on Ricalton).

35

Old family homes can be seen along Boyden Avenue from the bend in the road looking north toward Springfield Avenue. The view was taken *c.* 1913 before Harding and Brown Streets were cut through on the right.

This large house on Prospect Street near Burnett Terrace belonged to William H. Burnett, who was president of the Newark Realty Company, one of the early developers of the township. By 1910, the Newark Realty Company had possession of most of the Courter Farm and was developing it into an area called Mountain View Terrace. This area extended along the east side of Prospect Street from Tuscan Road to Madison Avenue.

Three

EDUCATION

Now a private residence at the corner of Ridgewood Road and Baker Street, this home, built in 1776 and called "Necessity Corner," was originally used as a tavern, meetinghouse, and store. George Washington is said to have visited here; and after the Revolutionary War, the dining room portion that has a small fireplace became the first school in Jefferson Village. Asher B. Durand was a pupil here at the beginning of the 19th century.

This small brick residence at 18 Tuscan Road, not far from today's Tuscan School, was built as the Vaux Hall School about 1838. It served as such until 1869 when the wooden school structure was erected on Maplewood Avenue, combining the districts of Vaux Hall and Jefferson Village.

About 1871, when the Maplewood School first opened, a photographer from Newark was hired to photograph the entire student body on the south lawn in front of the school, which was located where the Maplewood Post Office now stands. The first teachers, Miss Anna Dunnell (far right) and Miss Jane Courter (second from right), were from the old brick schoolhouse on Tuscan Road, and just preceded James Ricalton, the famous schoolmaster.

A beautiful, sunny day around 1900 brought out the majority of the student body for a formal photo session of the Maplewood School on Maplewood Avenue. Some of the pupils are identified in the photo below.

The members of Miss Juliaette Stewart's second-grade class at the Maplewood School in 1901, from left to right, are as follows: (front row) Russell Brown, Loretta Cogan, Elizabeth Chandler, unidentified, Hannah Heald, Mary Ricalton, Edna Miller, Natalie Kemp, Hattie Johnson, and Roger Pettit; (middle row) Jerome Gedney, unidentified, Everett Balch, Roy Thompson, Juliaette Stewart (teacher), two unidentified, Chester Sanford, Harold Balsover, and Watson Smith; (back row) Atlee O'Brien, Walter Gray, Lawrence Gedney, Harry Chandler, and Robert Brower.

The Middleville School was built in 1881 and in use until 1913. It stood on the corner of Boyden Avenue and Academy Street (now Tuscan Road). When the Seth Boyden School opened across the street in 1913, the old building had several new uses. Next to the school is the Hilton Methodist Church. The school was demolished, and the area now serves as a parking lot for the church.

The Seth Boyden School, an elementary school built in 1913, serves the Hilton section of the township. It is named after famous inventor Seth Boyden, who lived a few doors away from the school site from 1855 until he died in 1870.

Posed here in front of the entrance to the Seth Boyden School in 1921 is the graduating eighth-grade class. The owner of the picture, Gertrude Haas, is second from the left in the middle row.

A tank from World War II is on display at the rear of Fielding School in 1946. During World War II, patriotism was high in the elementary schools, with students doing whatever they could to help in the war effort: collecting newspapers, tin cans, and fat; knitting squares to make afghans for the Red Cross; purchasing Defense Stamps for as little as 10¢ each to buy U.S. Defense Savings Bonds; and helping in family victory gardens. Fielding School, built in 1914 and located on Academy Street, was named after Charles G. Fielding, president of the board of education. It served as an elementary school until it was closed in 1980; it is now the location of the South Orange-Maplewood Board of Education's central office.

This is an unusual view of the Maplewood School, also called Ricalton. It was built in 1902 and erected to replace the 1869 wooden building on the Maplewood Avenue-side of the railroad tracks. Ricalton School faced Baker Street, and it is now the oldest part of the present Maplewood Middle School. Notice the houses on the north side of Maple Avenue, which have since been moved or demolished.

Miss Weston's first-grade class at Ricalton School in 1911 is pictured here. The children in the photograph, listed from left to right and front to back, are as follows: (front row) Edward Scofield, Gus Timson, Helen McGinity, and Ruth Salter; (second row) Whitney Bird, Lealand Catlin, Dorothy Stafford, and Jannette McDonough; (third row) John Osmun, Paul Taylor, Dorothea Little, and Katherine Teller; (fourth row) Joseph Schlatz, Paul Renard, Honored Wells, and Evelyn Andrews; (fifth row) Henry Leslie, Herbert Ousterman, Irving Clark, and Dorothy Wilbur; (back row) Allister Moore, Alvin Amin, Sylvia Brushaber, and Virginia Hatch.

This postcard shows Maplewood Junior High School (now Maplewood Middle School) as it looked around 1940, when it was a school for grades seven through nine. Extensive additions to the original 1902 school were made to the southern portion, and the new entrance faced Burnet Street. More additions, including a new cafeteria and gymnasium, were made in the back in 1968.

Probably named after Governor DeWitt Clinton of New York, the Clinton School on Berkshire Road was finished in 1928 and serves as the elementary school for students in the northeastern section of the township.

The Jefferson School, located on Ridgewood Road and named after President Thomas Jefferson, was built as an elementary school in 1922. It is in the former Jefferson Village section of the township. Several additions have substantially enlarged the original school.

Here is a view of a 1938 kindergarten class in front of the entrance to the Jefferson School, which was then for grades K-6. What is most unusual are four sets of twins seated in the second row. In those days, children walked or rode bikes to school and went home for lunch.

44

Tuscan School, named after the legendary Native-American Chief Tuscan, was finished in time for elementary school classes to begin in the fall of 1924. Most of the teachers were from the Ricalton School on Baker Street, and most of them stayed for 20 years or more. Recently, a beautiful blend of architecture has been added to the north side.

Students at Tuscan School are acting out scenes honoring Chief Tuscan and his tribe as part of the celebration of our nation's bicentennial in 1976.

St. Joseph's School, the first parochial school in town, was built as an elementary school in 1930 on Franklin Avenue around the corner from St. Joseph's Church. Today, pupils in kindergarten through fourth grade are taught here.

The parish house of St. George's Episcopal Church on Clinton Avenue was used as a public school annex from 1922 to 1927 to relieve the overcrowded Ricalton School. Both the house and church were demolished after the present church was erected on the corner of Ridgewood Road and Woodland Road.

Scaffolding surrounding the new Columbia High School on January 24, 1927, shows the school is almost ready for opening. By that fall it was ready. Notice that a late-18th-century dwelling from the Beach Farm still survives at the front of the school. It was demolished soon after, however.

At a cost of $2 million, Columbia High School was finished in 1927 to serve students from both South Orange and Maplewood. Located at Parker Avenue and Valley Street, the school sits on the site of the former Beach Farm. The plans for the school were featured in the *Encyclopedia Britannica*.

The impressive entrance and tower of Columbia High School are shown in the late 1920s when the building was new. Note the awnings on the first-floor windows. The tower above the clock includes an observatory for sky watching.

Above the exit doors on both sides of the auditorium are carved owls. The owl was once Columbia's emblem, and it is still part of the logo for the South Orange-Maplewood Adult School. It is New Jersey's oldest adult school, with its office in Columbia High School. The beginning of a 1935 assembly is pictured in the beautiful Columbia High School auditorium with its pipe organ and leather-covered seats. Assemblies began with saluting the American flag and reading from the Old Testament of the Bible. In the 1940s, when Columbia High School was for grades 10–12, two identical assemblies were held every Friday morning.

Four

RELIGION

This meetinghouse on the corner of Bear Lane (now Claremont Avenue) and Ridgewood Road was the first church in Jefferson Village (now Maplewood). It was a Baptist chapel from its erection in 1812 until 1846. It was deeded to the Methodist Episcopal Church of Jefferson Village in 1858 and used by the Methodists at this location until 1890, when they moved it to Lenox Place. It is identified on Cyrus Durand's 1815 map (see p. 9) as "Babel Chapel," along with the first pastor, "Neighbor Joseph" Gildersleeve, who lived on Domini Street (now Jefferson Avenue).

This is a view of the inside of "Babel Chapel" on Children's Day, 1886. The lighting, which consisted of a lamp that hung from a hook attached to the ceiling, had been removed so the floral decoration could be photographed. The cross was covered with roses, and the gates were adorned with field daisies.

After the Methodists rolled the church down Ridgewood Road to Lenox Place, they added a vestibule and a bell tower. The bell in the "White Chapel" was used as the fire alarm for this part of town, so the vestibule door was always left open. After the death of John I. Morrow, who was pastor when the church was moved, the congregation named the church the Morrow Memorial Episcopal Church of Maplewood in 1897.

In 1911, the first stone section of the present Morrow Memorial United Methodist Church was built. The White Chapel, which can be seen behind the stone building, continued to be used as the Sunday school until 1926, when a large addition was made to the stone building.

In 1953, the cornerstone was put in place for the brick addition, known as Fellowship Hall, to the Morrow Memorial Church. A young Bill Burns in a dark robe can be seen intently watching. The Reverend Dr. William K. Burns served as the minister of music at the Morrow Memorial Church for 38 years.

The first Methodist church in town (the Hilton Methodist Church) was established in Middleville (now the Hilton section of Maplewood) in 1836. Middleville became Hilton in 1880 when it applied for a post office and found out there already was a Middleville Post Office in New Jersey. The Middleville School (to the left of the church) was torn down and is now the site of the church parking lot.

This is a woodcut of the Hilton Christian Church built in 1875. It became the First Congregational Christian Church of Maplewood in 1936. The church no longer exists.

The first St. George's Episcopal Church, built in 1895, was located on Clinton Avenue. It was constructed with cobblestones. Before this church was built, the services were held in the train depot since there were no trains on Sundays in the 1800s.

This is St. George's Episcopal Church on Ridgewood Road in the 1940s. The parish house, seen on the left behind the stone edifice, was built in 1921. Services were held there until 1926, when the stone structure was finished.

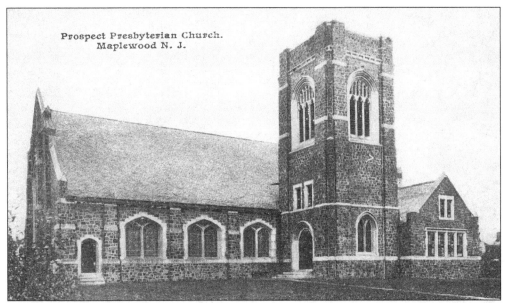

At the corner of Prospect Street and Tuscan Road, the Prospect Presbyterian Church is shown in this postcard *c.* 1926, when the present stone edifice was dedicated. In 1910, steps were taken to establish a Presbyterian church in Maplewood, and in 1912 a small chapel (no longer in existence) was completed. In 1946, a large, stained-glass window, visible today on the Prospect Street side (to the far left in the photograph), was dedicated to those who served in World War II.

The Gospel Chapel was built in 1938 on the corner of Burnet and Lexington Avenues by a congregation independent of any established denomination. The architecture is similar to the early New England meetinghouses.

In 1927, Lutherans organized and met in the Jefferson School. A year later they assembled at Fielding School. Finally on May 8, 1938, they dedicated this attractive church building at the corner of Parker Avenue and Burr Road. The Lutherans celebrated the burning of their mortgage in 1948.

Near the corner of Parker Avenue and Prospect Street, the Calvary Reformed Church was built in 1927. The congregation changed its name to the Calvary Community Church in 1959. After a disastrous fire on March 20, 1976, the church was rebuilt. Today, three different religions share the sanctuary.

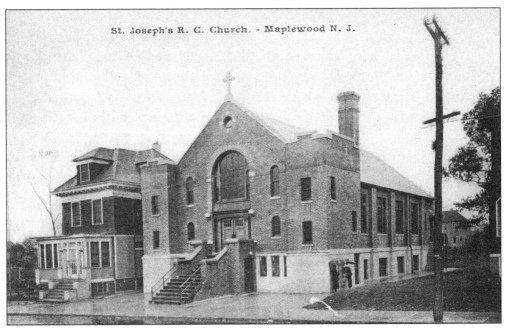

St. Joseph's Church, founded in 1914, was organized by parishioners from Newark. Shown here is the original church, built in 1922, which stood on the site of the present church.

The congregation of the Immaculate Heart of Mary Parish, founded in 1954, is shown here celebrating its 25th anniversary. The steeply pitched, laminated wood arches and sanctuary lighting emphasize the marble altar.

Five

LEGENDARY CITIZENS

On Flag Day, Sunday, June 14, 1959,
nine murals painted in the wall panels
of the meeting room of the Maplewood
Municipal Building were dedicated.
They were painted by Hungarian-born
Stephen Juharos. Shown here is the
artist putting the finishing touches
on the first panel. It shows a scene of
one of Maplewood's first dwellers, the
legendary Chief Tuscan, who lived
along the banks of the brook just south
of Tuscan Road.

Here is Asher Brown Durand (1796–1886), shown with his easel and landscape painting. It was done by Daniel Huntington in 1857 during Durand's middle years, when he was painting landscapes directly from nature and was considered a founder of the Hudson River school of painting (see p. 15 for more on Asher Durand).

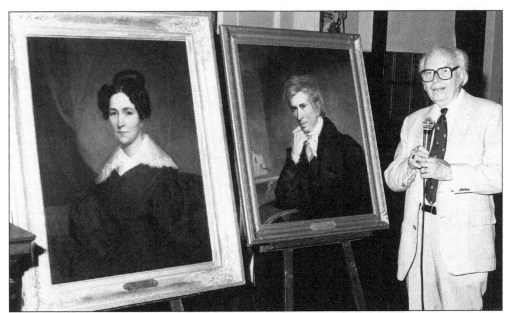

Joseph Veach Noble, a prominent art historian and Maplewood resident, is giving a lecture about Cyrus Durand (the older brother of Asher) and his wife, when their portraits were presented to the Durand-Hedden House and Garden Association in the town hall. The portraits were painted by Asher B. Durand about 1830 and are currently hanging in the Victorian parlor of the Durand-Hedden House.

Carol Van Ness Casey sits at the desk that belonged to his great uncle, James Van Ness, a pioneer citizen of the Hilton area. Caleb Van Ness, the father of James, is shown above the desk. Andrew Jackson Van Ness, another son of Caleb, was the founder of the Maplewood library system, his books being the nucleus of the Hilton Library volumes.

Seth Boyden (1788–1870) settled in Middleville in 1855 after starting several successful industries in Newark as a result of his inventions. He made the first malleable iron, the first two steam engines for the Morris & Essex Railroad, daguerreotypes (photographs), and patent leather. While here, Boyden cultivated the huge "Hilton Strawberries," which brought prosperity to the Hilton farmers. At a ceremony honoring Seth Boyden in 1926, Thomas Edison said, "Seth Boyden was one of America's greatest inventors, and one who had never received proper credit for his many great and practical inventions. They have been the basis of great industries, which have spread over the entire world and given employment to millions of people." (Quotation from Bulletin No. 10, 1939–40 series of New Jersey Writers' Project, Work Projects Administration.)

In 1871, Professor James Ricalton (1844–1929) was hired as Maplewood's first permanent schoolmaster. While schoolmaster from 1871 to 1891, he spent his summers traveling the world. In 1888, he took a leave of absence to search the world for the best bamboo to use as a filament in Thomas Edison's newly invented light bulb. Eventually, Ricalton left his teaching career to become a full-time professional photographer, world traveler, and war correspondent. He traveled over 500,000 miles, took 100,000 photographs (many stereographs), and tested Edison's new movie camera, shooting 30 miles of film. In this photo, taken by himself c. 1890, Ricalton is atop the Great Pyramid of Cheops in Egypt.

Theodore Roosevelt (1858–1919) spent summer months at his uncle and aunt's estate, "The Hickories," in the hills west of Ridgewood Road during the late 1860s and early 1870s. Young Theodore was frail and suffered from asthma. He would travel from his boyhood home in New York City to spend time in Maplewood, where he could pursue his interests in wild animals, birds, and plants.

Pictured here are Theodore Roosevelt's aunt and uncle, Laura and Cornelius Van Schaick Roosevelt. Their Maplewood estate, called "The Hickories," was built in 1865 and was their home during the six warm months every year until 1900. Cornelius died in the Maplewood house in 1887, and Laura continued to live there until 1900, when she died at their home in New York City.

Author Agnes Sligh Turnbull (1888–1982) was a longtime resident of Maplewood. Initially an English teacher, she wrote short stories from 1918 until 1936, when her first novel, *The Rolling Years*, was published. Many popular novels followed, including a bestseller in 1947, *The Bishop's Mantle*. She also wrote nonfiction and books for children. In this photo, she is working at her desk in her home on Claremont Avenue in Maplewood. (Photo by Richard's Studio.)

This photograph shows Harriet Stratemeyer Adams (1892–1982), a well-known Maplewood author of more than 200 books, receiving recognition from Mayor Robert Grasmere in 1978. Harriet Adams, who wrote under several pen names, wrote the 55 books in the Nancy Drew mystery series for young readers, including rewriting (using the pen name of Carolyn Keene) the first three drafts written by her father, Edward Stratemeyer.

The man in the center of this photograph, Dr. William Lowell, invented the golf tee in 1921. That was the year he switched from playing tennis to playing golf at the Maplewood Country Club. He resisted using the 400-year-old tradition in golf of forming a mound of wet sand to tee the ball, so he whittled the first wooden golf tee. He got a patent, and his two sons (Ernest Lowell on the left and William Lowell Jr. on the right) established a company to manufacture golf tees. Dr. Lowell built his home at 12 Lenox Place in 1904.

Six

TRANSPORTATION

In 1902, the railroad tracks were elevated, and in 1904 the old Maplewood School became the town hall. The passenger train pulled by a steam engine is shown heading east toward New York City about to pass the building that was the Maplewood Town Hall until 1932, when it became the library.

MORRIS & ESSEX RAILROAD.

THIS road was chartered January 29th, 1835, and the Company commenced running their Cars by horse power from Newark to Orange November 19th, 1836; from Newark to Madison by steam power on Monday the second of October, 1837; and from Newark to Morristown on the first day of January, 1838. The average daily receipts from Newark to Morristown (for passengers) from first of January to first of May, has been $72. An eight wheel Car, capable of carrying from seventy to one hundred passengers, was placed on the road the 15th February, 1838, and a second engine was put on the road in May, 1838. The Cars now leave Newark and Morristown three times a day. The road has also been surveyed from Morristown to Easton, and is expected to be under contract this summer—and from thence to Carpenter's Point.

Summer Arrangements.

Leaves Newark	6¼ A. M.	Leaves Morristown	6¼ A.M.
"	10 "	" "	1¼ P.M
"	5 P. M.	" "	5 "

Fare.

Newark to Orange	12¼	Newark to Chatham	50
" S. Orange	25	" Madison	62¼
" Millville	31¼	" Morristown	75
" Summit	44		

When the Morris & Essex Railroad had this schedule printed in 1838, the Old Stone House in Jefferson Village (now Maplewood) was a flag stop. The arrangement continued until a platform was built on the west side of the tracks and on the south side of Baker Street in 1859. The first station was built the following year.

The first railroad depot in town was built in 1860 on the west side of the tracks, just south of Baker Street. A name was needed, and Mrs. Elijah Gardner suggested "Maplewood," a name that has endured through the rest of the township's history. When the present station was built in 1902, the old depot was moved a few feet to Baker Street and for a short while became a shoe store.

To the left is the Maplewood School in the distance. This photograph shows how close the building was to the tracks of the Morris & Essex Railroad. Occasionally, the pupils were disturbed by the train noise. The view is looking north toward South Orange from the Baker Street crossing. The scene is about 1890, before the tracks were elevated and before the present station was built in 1902.

Here is another view of the Baker Street grade crossing, looking east toward Valley Street from Maplewood Avenue c. 1890.

This postcard illustrates the present railroad station built in 1902. In the lower right it says, "from Papa," who mailed it in New York City to his son, Master H.H.S. Phillips, at 9 Clinton Avenue. The New York City postmark on the address side, which in those days could not contain any message, is October 6, 1905. The receiving postmark on the picture side is Maplewood, October 7. The cost of postage was 1¢. A horse and buggy are waiting for passengers, and no automobiles are fighting for a parking space.

Summer was a favorite time to enjoy a ride in the country. Here are four children and two ladies of the Bodei family getting ready to tell the horse to pull the surrey with the fringe on top. This photograph was probably taken in the early 1900s.

This open-air trolley, used in the warm weather, is at the passing track on Valley Street (in front of the present town hall). The car belongs to the Consolidation Traction Company, *c.* 1900.

These two trolleys are about to pass each other in opposite directions at the same spot on Valley Street as the trolley in the photograph above. One of the trolleys has to stop on the passing track and wait for the other to pass it on the main track before it can switch back to the main track and proceed. These two *c.* 1915 cars belonged to Public Service.

Here is Maplewood's first traffic jam. Two White steam cars, both owned by the Riker family of Mountain Avenue, are trying to pass each other in the South Mountain Reservation about 1907. Clarence B. Riker is standing in the car on the left; his son, Carleton Riker Sr., is at the wheel of the car on the right. (Courtesy of Carleton B. Riker Jr.)

Everett P. Balch, behind the wheel of a 1905 White steam car, is giving a ride to his friend Donald Munsick about 1910. At the beginning of the automobile age, steamers were more popular than gas-driven automobiles. This is a photograph of the second car owned by Edward C. Balch and Harry N. Balch. (Courtesy of Peter B. Sickley and Robert C. Sickley Jr.)

One of the last runs of a steam locomotive on the Delaware, Lackawanna and Western Railroad took place on April 9, 1931. Here the locomotive is bellowing its way through town on its way to Millburn, along the southern end of Maplewood Avenue.

Commuters are boarding a train heading for Hoboken in the morning sunshine about 1946. The 1902 station is shown in the distance on the left.

Thomas A. Edison (second from the left) inaugurates the first electrified rail service on the Morris & Essex line of the Lackawanna on September 3, 1930. This photograph was taken in Hoboken before the train left for Maplewood.

September 1984 is when the railroad re-electrified with new cars. Shown here in the leading car of the train to celebrate the event are, from left to right, Tom Keene, Robert Klein, Ed Borrone, Mayor Robert Grasmere (representing Maplewood's township committee), and Thomas Edison Sloane (the great-grandson of Thomas Edison).

Seven

PROTECTION

The first policeman in town made his rounds on horseback. The sign on the left reads, "Automobiles Go Slow. Speed Limit Enforced In This Township." Are the children in the go-cart obeying the law? The scene is along Prospect Street about 1907.

The career of Jake Helf is shown on these two pages. Above is Helf at the wheel of an early automobile as a chauffeur about 1910.

A few years later, Helf is seen as a patrolman on an Excelsior Auto-Cycle in back of police headquarters.

Thirteen members of the 1916 police force posed in uniform for this photograph. Jake Helf is easily identified at the right, holding on to his motorcycle.

By 1920, Jake Helf was chief of police. He is shown here (extreme right) with his 24 men in front of headquarters, the former Maplewood School that later became the library on Maplewood Avenue.

South Orange Heights was a section of town north of Tuscan Road and east of Prospect Street. For a short while, this area had its own hose company. Shown here are 14 firemen of that company in their best attire, white gloves and all, in front of the barn where they kept their hose and reel around 1900.

Posing in front of the Hilton Firehouse are 15 proud men, probably getting ready for the Fourth of July parade. It is amusing that the second floor of the firehouse was the headquarters of the Hilton Pleasure Club c. 1900.

One of the spectacular fires in town about 1917 was the burning of Le Bret's Garage on Dunnell Road near the location of the present fire headquarters. Also observed was the performance of the new fire engine, shown in the foreground.

Built in 1924 on the site of the Dunnell Paper Mill (see p. 92), the fire department headquarters has space for four engines and also sleeping rooms on the second floor. Another firehouse is located in the Hilton section of town.

Labeled "Municipal Building, Hilton, N.J." on this postcard, the first floor of this building housed the fire department for the Hilton part of what is now Maplewood. The second floor was the Hilton Library.

This souvenir badge of September 25, 1912, illustrates the Hilton Firehouse. Attached is a small metal fireman's helmet. It belonged to George Michael Haas (1873–1943) of Boyden Avenue.

All dressed up in uniform are members of the Maplewood Volunteer Fire Department *c.* 1910. The photograph was taken in front of their new firehouse on Maplewood Avenue just south of where the post office is now. This first hook and ladder apparatus, built by the Cope Wagon Manufacturing Co. (see p. 96), was drawn by either horse or man.

In 1913, the same hook and ladder was attached to a new motor truck. The first paid firemen were the drivers. The Hilton Firehouse received its first motor apparatus in 1917. When the present headquarters was built in 1924 on Dunnell Road, all firemen went on a full-paid status.

This Civil Defense Disaster Truck was constructed in 1941 entirely of second-hand material. It was equipped with a 10,000-watt electric power unit, an air compressor, an acetylene torch and cutting unit, and a water pump.

Auxiliary Fire Engine No. 4 of the Maplewood Civilian Defense Council was one of the units of auxiliary fire equipment placed at various locations throughout the town in 1942. During World War II, the fire auxiliary consisted of volunteers who met weekly for training and were drilled on firefighting procedures to be used in case of an air raid.

Eight

PUBLIC USE

Assembled in the old Middleville School are members of the Hilton Reading Club, which was organized in March 1882. Andrew J. Van Ness acquired books for schoolchildren, and his library became the nucleus of the Hilton branch of the public library. The members, from left to right, are as follows: (front row) Andrew J. Van Ness, Louis Becker, Laura Osborn, Mrs. Charles Stewart, Fannie Evans, and Joseph H. Osborn; (back row) five unidentified men.

Built as the Maplewood School in 1869, this building was vacated as a school after the Ricalton School was built in 1902. It became the town hall from 1904 to 1932. Next it became the Maplewood Free Public Library until the present Maplewood Memorial Library was erected in Memorial Park.

This oil painting by Karl Egge of the former school, town hall, and library was executed after the building was demolished to make room for the present post office. The painting is framed by pieces of wood from the old edifice and hangs in the mayor's office.

The Maplewood Municipal Building was dedicated in 1931 on the site of the Wesley Van Iderstine House and part of the estate of Henry S. Smith. The decorations of bunting and crowds of people denote opening day.

Noted for its classic simplicity and beauty, the Municipal Building is the symbol of the township. The meetingroom walls contain magnificent murals, depicting the history and development of Maplewood.

Not having a place of its own, the library, founded in April 1913, was housed in the basement of the Ricalton School (now the Maplewood Middle School) across the street from the present library. Wicker furniture was the rage, and statues of Julius Caesar and the Venus de Milo are looking down from the top of the bookcase.

To help bring back memories, here is the main desk in the center hallway of the library, when it occupied the former schoolhouse on Maplewood Avenue. When the photograph was taken in the fall of 1943, patrons were dreaming of a new building once World War II was over.

From the air, one can see the construction of the present library during 1955 and 1956, across the street from the Maplewood Junior High School (now the Maplewood Middle School), where the first home of the library was located.

This beautiful scene is a view of the completed library located in Memorial Park facing Baker Street. The photograph was taken before the library was enlarged. Many homes were removed from this location during the 1920s to create the park.

Enthusiastic pre-schoolers of the 1960s are pictured here coming from story hour through the hidden bookcase door in the Children's Room of the Maplewood Memorial Library. The open bookcase door can be seen at the end of the line of children.

Similar in architectural design, the Hilton branch of the library was constructed a few blocks west of its old location (see p. 78) on Springfield Avenue. The south end of the building houses a health clinic and a police substation.

The Woman's Club of Maplewood has a very impressive building, which was erected in 1930. The club was founded in 1916 and federated in 1917. Located on Woodland Road near Maplewood Center, the clubhouse is used for many other organizations' meetings and special events, such as wedding receptions.

Around the corner from the Woman's Club is the Burgdorff Cultural Center on Durand Road. Built as the First Church of Christ Scientist in 1925, this building is a good example of French Normandy architecture. When the congregation disbanded, Jean Burgdorff, a local realtor, purchased the building and gave it to the town as a civic and cultural center. Maplewood's well-known theater group, The Strollers, is the resident theater company (see p. 125).

The historic Durand-Hedden House and Garden is located in Grasmere Park on Ridgewood Road. The original farmhouse, built in the late 18th century, and the surrounding 2 acres of the park are now owned by the Township of Maplewood. The award-winning educational herb garden in the foreground is maintained by the Maplewood Garden Club. The garden, which has one of the largest herb collections in the northeast, is open daily. (Photo by Peter Sickles.)

This front view of the Durand-Hedden House from Ridgewood Road shows the two sections of the house, reflecting two different periods of construction. The section on the left, with a brick beehive bake oven in the center of the south side, was built in the late 18th century. The center section (right) was added in the mid-19th century. The house is maintained by the Durand-Hedden House and Garden Association.

The kitchen is the focal point of the Durand-Hedden House. Every month during the open house, food preparation is carefully demonstrated, and visitors get to taste the results. Docents, or teachers, are dressed in period costume and demonstrate cooking in the *c.* 1790 fireplace. On the left is Rachel Gruenberg and at the right is Irene Kosinski.

This is a photograph of the 19th-century parlor at the Durand-Hedden House before authentic restoration to the Victorian period, when it was built. Carolyn Zipps is standing in front of the fireplace. The mirror has been replaced with a painting of Cyrus Durand (see p. 59). In addition to the monthly open house, group tours for schoolchildren and others are scheduled by appointment.

The Maplewood Garden Club greenhouse resulted from an interest within the community in victory gardening during World War II. In 1947, the club members voted to sponsor the building of a greenhouse. The Town provided land behind the Municipal Building, and the members raised money for materials and built it themselves! Walter Smith and Keith Kinyon are making finishing touches in time for the December 1948 opening.

Shown here is a horse-drawn snowplow clearing the sidewalk along Baker Street around 1910. This made it easier for commuters to reach the train station. The Ricalton School (now the Maplewood Middle School) is on the left. The houses on the right were removed when Memorial Park was created.

Nine

BUSINESS

The present Maplewood Center was still farmland and woods in 1841, when this store was built by Aaron Crowell on the Crowell Farm on Valley Street, where Park Road is today. At this point in history, Jefferson Village was part of Springfield Township, and this area east of Valley Street was part of Clinton Township. The store, which was called the "Clinton Valley Store and Shoe Manufactory," was also the branch post office for South Orange after 1861. Harry J. Baker was a clerk in this store before he bought the business and moved it to Baker Street in 1888. This photograph was probably taken in 1870.

This is the Dunnell Paper Mill in 1870. It was located at the foot of Oakland Road, approximately where the fire department headquarters is today. In the early 1800s, it was a woolen mill. Mr. Dunnell bought it in 1837 and converted it to be used for the manufacture of manila paper, commonly used as wrapping paper in grocery stores. Twenty people lost their jobs when the mill burned down in 1892.

The Crowell Cider Mill was a well-known attraction in the 1800s. It was located on Valley Street near Crowell Road (now Parker Avenue). Until 1884, the apple-grinding was done in the basement, using horses that were harnessed to a long pole attached to the sweep. They walked in a continuous circle around the sweep. The cider mill went out of existence in 1919.

Pierson's Mill was built in 1831 by Lewis Pierson and has been a familiar landmark ever since. The gristmill was operated by waterpower from a man-made pond fed by the east branch of the Rahway River until 1909.

In 1890, this is how the corner of Baker Street and Maplewood Avenue looked. Harry Baker's store is the first building on the left with an awning over the store entrance.

By 1920, the corner of Baker Street and Maplewood Avenue shows signs of a developing center. More stores can be seen, and electric utility poles with street lighting have been added.

This postcard mailed in 1906 shows Harry Baker's store with a horse and buggy in front. The recently elevated railroad overpass is in the distance at the right. The small building to the left of the overpass is the old depot, relocated from its original location at the foot of Lenox Place. In 1906, messages could only be written on the front of postcards. The sender of this one is telling her friend that she lives on the second floor of the house on the corner of Baker Street and Maplewood Avenue.

H. J. BAKER
DEALER IN
FANCY AND STAPLE GROCERIES
Delicious Creamery Butter a Specialty.

ALL THE LEADING BRANDS OF
CANNED GOODS, CALIFORNIA FRUITS IN TIN. FRUITS—ORANGES. LEMONS, BANANAS AND COCOANUTS.

HIGH GRADE TEAS AND COFFEES.
ALL THE
LEADING BRANDS OF FLOUR.
HOLMES & COUTS' AND KENNEDY'S FAMOUS BISCUITS

ORDERS CALLED FOR AND DELIVERED DAILY, FREE OF CHARGE.

Baker Street, - - Maplewood, N. J.

In 1890, Maplewood had only one store in the center, which was located on Baker Street and owned by Harry J. Baker, who was also the postmaster. He carried most groceries, except meat, which was supplied by George W. Eager from a meat wagon that traveled around town several times a week.

95

The Cope Company, which manufactured wagons and carriages, was located on the corner of Springfield Avenue and Boyden Avenue. It was Hilton's biggest industry from 1887 until it burned down.

The Hilton Post Office was established in 1880 in Charles Stewart's store at the corner of Springfield Avenue and Burnett Avenue.

This is a photograph of horse-drawn milk delivery wagons struggling to get through the heavy snow on one of the main roads (probably Springfield Avenue), *c.* 1912.

This is a view of the Public Service car barns (bus terminal) on Springfield Avenue near Boyden Avenue in 1913. Notice the trolley tracks embedded in the roadway.

As one can see in the picture, the Woolley Coal Company also delivered ice to Maplewood in the days before refrigeration.

Shown here is an early horse-drawn open wagon used for delivering coal.

This is one of Woolley's Ford Model T coal delivery trucks. Horses were no longer required, but manpower was still needed to crank the engine to get it started.

This is a view of Woolley's Coal and Fuel Oil Company in 1942.

Samuel H. Ross, Inc. started its meat market and grocery store on Maplewood Avenue in 1905. In that year, the population of the township was 1,946. Until Samuel Ross incorporated a butcher shop in his grocery store, the community had been served by "roving butcher peddlers."

Twenty-five years later we see a picture of the new, enlarged store building owned by S.H. Ross. The gasoline-driven delivery truck parked in front replaced the first delivery wagon and "Dobbin" (the horse).

This is a view of the village looking north on Maplewood Avenue from Baker Street in the early 1920s. To the left of the car headed south, one can see a gasoline pump used for refueling cars. It looks like a dark column anchored to the sidewalk with a circular white-glass ornament on top.

This is another view of Maplewood Village looking north from the intersection of Baker Street and Maplewood Avenue. On the right-hand corner, Fraentzel's Hardware Store, established in 1912, was in business on the first floor with the Masonic Hall located on the second floor of the brick building.

Moving north on Maplewood Avenue just above Highland Place, one can see that the village is still not fully developed with stores. The house on the left stands proudly right next to a group of storefronts. There also seems to be ample parking space.

Another view, looking north on Maplewood Avenue, shows that on the left, above Inwood Place, there was still a wooded area.

Nelson's Garage, established in 1912, has been a familiar sight to train commuters and car owners since the early part of the 20th century. This automotive repair shop is located on Dunnell Road near the train station.

A familiar sight on Springfield Avenue is Wyman Ford, the oldest car dealer in Maplewood that is still in business.

This is Maplewood Village looking south on Maplewood Avenue from Inwood Place, *c.* 1923. In the center of the photograph, one can still see houses that have been converted into stores.

Ten
EVENTS

This scene occurred on Memorial Day, 1896, in front of the Hilton Hotel during the annual Irvington to Millburn bicycle race. The hotel was located on the north side of Springfield Avenue at the intersection of Tuscan Road.

Shown here is an enlarged copy of a fragile, badly deteriorated frame from a Thomas Edison movie of the 1915 Fourth of July Celebration. In *Maplewood Past and Present*, Mrs. Harcourt remembers, "One Fourth I remember there were about 11 automobiles on the Field Club grounds with headlights turned on (probably oil), so the few young people could dance on the green."

This is another frame from the Thomas Edison movie of the 1915 Fourth of July, viewing the parade on Maplewood Avenue from the foot of Lenox Place. Pictured is the neighborhood entry representing the Blue Ridge Park section on the east side of Valley Street near Pierson's Mill.

The parade float coming down Maplewood Avenue in this photograph is the "Ridgewood Terrace Short Line 515," built by the residents of Ridgewood Terrace. It won first prize in the 1915 Fourth of July Parade.

A 1916 Fourth of July Parade float depicting an airship named "America" is seen here at the corner of Maplewood Avenue and Baker Street. This was another achievement of the Ridgewood Terrace "engineers."

This Fourth of July parade entry was called the "Jitney Express." Harold Thompson and Lloyd Roberts were driving the express that the hen appears to be pulling. It is said that the hen went on strike in the middle of Maplewood Center and held up the parade.

Pictured here is train car 802, which was part of the Ridgewood Terrace Short Line float shown on the previous page. The flagpole on Wyoming Avenue at the head of Ridgewood Terrace symbolizes the pride that the residents of Ridgewood Terrace took in the success of their parade entries.

MAPLEWOOD YESTERDAY AND TODAY

Illustrated Talk by ARTHUR V. FARR

A Series of
Slides will
Illustrate
the Talk

All Residents
Invited—

Ladies
Welcome

The Story of Changing Maplewood from the Days of the Indians up to the Present

This rare broadside is an advertisement for a glass lantern slide show given in the Maplewood School Auditorium (now the Maplewood Middle School) at 8:30 p.m. on October 18, 1915. It was sponsored by the Maplewood Improvement Association, which became the Maplewood Civic Association. Many of the glass slides have survived and have been used recently in historical presentations.

This patriotic scene took place on the Fourth of July, 1918, behind the Field Club on Baker Street. Two hundred military men in World War I took part in the program. There were 100 soldiers from Camp Dix and 100 sailors from a United States warship. The estimated attendance at the exercises was 4,000.

Floods occasionally caused the east branch of the Rahway River to overflow near the Field Club on Baker Street. This photograph shows the rampant water trying to get under the Baker Street bridge.

Sometimes traffic through Maplewood Village would get tied up by a flood. This is a view looking north toward the intersection of Maplewood Avenue and Highland Place.

Here is a view of the flood on Baker Street at the foot of Burnet Street looking toward Louis Cracco's house and the Field Club building. The license plate on the car is dated 1915.

In September 1931, Memorial Park was dedicated to the men and women who served their country in World War I. Standing, from left to right, are H.C. Brown, J.S. DeHart (chairman of the township committee), W.H. Kemp, Colonel Tench (veteran of the Civil War and honored guest), and Caswell Heine.

On April 24, 1950, the Columbia High School Class of 1900 celebrated its 50th reunion, and over 50% of the class attended. Singing the Columbia High "Alma Mater," from left to right, are Edith Witthuhn, Alice Fleming (Homer's wife), Carro Terry McAdams, Edna Smalley Ward, Edna Ward Pryor, Jessie Smith Zellers, Charlotte Crowell Salter, and Homer Fleming (at the piano).

This photograph is of the cornerstone laying for Maplewood Memorial Library in 1955. Those present, from left to right, were William Santoro (president of the library board of trustees), Mayor Thomas W. Sweeney, and Township Committeeman George M. Wallhauser (who chaired the library building committee).

On May 24, 1959, the present building of the Hilton branch of the Maplewood Memorial Library was dedicated. Standing, from left to right, are Howard W. Wiseman (assistant head of the New Jersey Historical Society), Mary L. Hetherington (librarian), and Thomas W. Sweeney (mayor). Seated on the right is Helen V.D. Winter, director of the Maplewood Memorial Library.

Dignitaries at the opening ceremonies of Maplewood's Dickens Village in 1961 were, from left to right, Sheldon O'Dell (mayor), O.Vincent McNany (Maplewood postmaster), Sir G.A.J. Boon (British council general in New York City), Mathew Clark (British Travel Agency), and Robert H. Grasmere (president of the Maplewood Chamber of Commerce and chairman of Dickens Village Foundation). Pictured in the inset is part of the parade coming up Maplewood Avenue in authentic costumes of the Dickens era of the mid-19th century.

Memorial Day, May 25, 1981, was the occasion for the Maplewood Civic Association (MCA) to celebrate in Memorial Park. Representing the organization, from left to right, are Clifford Freeman, Jack Warner, Charlotte Mathias, and Rudy Mathias. The MCA was founded in 1905 and is responsible for Maplewood's Fourth of July celebration, the Maple Leaf Award, the Citizens Budget Advisory Committee, and many other civic programs.

In 1961, Maplewood and South Orange celebrated the centennial of the formation of South Orange Township from Clinton Township and Orange Town. In 1861, South Orange Township included both Maplewood and what became the Village of South Orange. The Jefferson Village part of Maplewood was still part of Millburn Township until 1863.

The Maplewood Country Club was the scene of the Bicentennial Ball in 1976, commemorating the signing of the Declaration of Independence. Assembled in front of the fireplace, the township committee members, from left to right, are as follows: (seated) Edward J. Borrone, Mayor Robert H. Grasmere, and Vice Mayor Robert C. Klein; (standing) John F. Blanchard (chairman of the bicentennial committee) and Michael D. DeCicco (member of the township committee).

On Memorial Day, May 25, 1981, Mayor Robert H. Grasmere addressed citizens in front of the Maplewood Memorial Library during the dedication of a bronze plaque in sacred memory of Maplewoodians who gave their lives in the service of our country in 20th-century wars.

IN SACRED MEMORY

WORLD WAR I

HENRY P. BUSH	CHARLES D. NELSON	CHARLES H. THOMSON
RALPH J.G. LANE	ROBERT G. STOKELY	RENNIE G. VAN HOUTON
GEORGE H. MANLEY		STEPHEN R. WARNER

WORLD WAR II

RUSSELL V. ADAMS, JR.	IRVING A. FEIGENBAUM	HENRY B. MALONE, JR.
JOSEPH G. ANDRES	THEODORE F. FETTINGER	DURAND R. MEARNS
VINCENT J. BARBA	BOUTWELL H. FOSTER, JR.	NELSON L. MILLAR
CHARLES J. BECHT, JR.	PAUL W. FRANK	PAUL B. MULLER
CHAS. W. BENFIELD, JR.	ARNOLD E. FRITZ	RICHARD A. MURPHY
WILLIAM E. BOLSOVER	VIBERT O. FRYER	HUGH K. MYERS
GEORGE A. BOWEN	GEORGE W. GEE	C. BRADFORD NICKEL
JOHN J. BROWN	LAWRENCE GRASHA	ERLING C. OLSEN
JOHN J. BURKHARDT	RUSSELL J.W. HALLER	ERNEST A. PENNELL, JR.
HENRY S. CABALLERO	EDWARD J. HANLEY, JR.	R. WAYNE PERKINS
WILLIAM J. CAMERON, JR.	CORLY W. HANSEN, JR.	AMOS A. PLANTE
NILS T. CARLSON	BARRY HAVILAND	HAROLD PRINCE
JOSEPH B. CHRISTOPH	LEO C. HAZMUKA	JOHN F. PURCELL
RICHARD B. CLANCY	WILLIAM C. HELLMUND	ROBERT D. RODGERS
ALAN CLARK	HARRISON HIGHAM	CHARLES R. ROSSO
FRANK C. COAKLEY	ROBERT F. HOFFMANN	GEORGE A. RYNAR
DAVID K. CROKER	ROBERT J. HUFF	HECTOR V. SCALA
HAROLD L. CROSS, JR.	RICHARD C. HURLBURT	WESLEY C. SCHEIDER
JOHN H. CUNNINGHAM	HUBERT HUTCHINSON, JR.	ROBERT J. SCHUBERT
JOHN N. DARLING	WALTER L. IBSCHER	GLENDON S. SEIFERT
ROBERT L. DE GROFF	EDWARD H. INSINGER	ROBERT C. SEITZMEYER
JAMES E. DENNISSON	EDWARD A. JANTZEN	HARRY E. SHANKLIN
FRANK J. DEVLIN	FRANCIS X. JOYCE	RICHARD S. SMITH
KENNETH B. DIAS	THEODORE L. KASALKA	JOSEPH J. SOMMER
ROBERT H. DIETZE	BERNARD D. KENO	PAUL A. SOMMERS
CHARLES R. DRAKE, JR.	LEONARD A. KEYES, JR.	WILLIAM R. SPEIRS
RUSSELL L. EDGECOMBE	LOUIS KINSKY, JR.	GEORGE O. TICHENOR
EDWARD P. ELLIS	FRED D. LANG	WILLIAM H. VOELLMICKE
ROBERT B. ERNEST	JACK LARSEN	ROBERT F. VOGEL
RAYMOND G. ERRINGTON	LESTER P. LARSON	JOHN A. WALSH
ANNA J. EVANS	JAMES A. LEMMER	WILLIAM J. WARRING, JR.
CLIFFORD B. EVANS	ALBERT L. LUTHER	RUSSELL W. WEIDELE
EDWARD V. FARRELL	ROBERT S. MAC NABB	FREDERICK K. WENZEL
	SAMUEL N. MACE	

KOREAN WAR

GUSTAVE LUDDEKE, JR.	JULIUS J. STUDENY	WALLACE C. SWOPE
DONALD WATSON SALMON		STANLEY WRIGHT, JR.

VIETNAM WAR

ROBERT W. ANDREASEN	DANIEL J. HEFFERNAN	MICHAEL J. LAWRENCE
RUSSELL H. CORNISH		GREGORY J. MC INTYRE

This memorial plaque lists the names of those Maplewood men and women who lost their lives in World War I, World War II, the Korean War, and the Vietnam War. One hundred were killed in World War II alone. The plaque is located in the foyer of the Maplewood Memorial Library.

The township committee celebrates the Fourth of July by riding in a 1911 Stevens Duryea driven by Norman Woolley of the fuel company. Mayor Robert Grasmere is in front with the driver, and Robert Klein (left) and Edward Lynott (right) are in the back seat.

Eleven

RECREATION

In 1904, a popular form of recreation was the church social. This one was at the home of Mrs. H. Reeve on Mountain Avenue. Among the guests are Mrs. George Low, Mrs. E.C. Balch, Misses Ida and Alice Carpenter, Mrs. Clarence Riker, Mrs. Harry Baker, Mrs. May Balch Summers, and Mrs. John Le Count. Also present was a very young Donald Summers, who became the chemistry teacher at Columbia High School known as "Doc" Summers.

This winter scene is a view of Pierson's Pond looking east toward Valley Street in 1900. The man-made pond, which was created by Lewis Pierson in 1831, remained a popular spot for ice skating until it was drained in 1916. The house at the far right belonged to James Ricalton.

The present man-made pond for ice skating is located in Memorial Park. This is a view looking north toward the police headquarters and the railroad. The snow and ice suggest a good season during which the sign on the tree probably stayed up most of the time. (Photo by Sickles Photo-Reporting Service.)

When the area was still rural, Labor Day in 1891 seemed like a good time to have a shooting tournament for amateurs only. The program boldly states, "Experts Barred."

This group of men is posing for the photographer at the third annual clambake of the Maplewood Sporting Club on July 31, 1904. The chef (at the far right) is ready to serve the hungry sportsmen.

The South Orange YMCA, which included Maplewood members, is resting between innings of a baseball game about 1900. The player second from the right in the top row is Edward M. Van Iderstine, who lived on Valley Street near Oakview Avenue.

The photograph of this handsome baseball team was taken on June 7, 1902. The players, from left to right, are as follows: (seated in front) Everett Balch and Edgar Fielding; (standing) Benjamin Nathan, R.L. Smith, G. Russell Salter, Howard Cheshire, Philip Karcher, Raymond Barnard, Howard M. Crowell, Howard Gardner, Charlie Edwards, and Leander Mosher. In the back by the tree is Nason Toulon.

Mrs. George M. Haas of Boyden Avenue was within walking distance of Olympic Park. She was able to enjoy the season pass during the 1965–66 golden anniversary of this landmark amusement park.

The Public Service Railway, in 1916, advertised Olympic Park on the Irvington-Maplewood border as a place for fun. Shown here is the entrance to the park and the trolley that would take one there.

The Maplewood Field Club, predecessor to the Maplewood Country Club, stood right on the edge of Baker Street near the site of the present clubhouse. This photograph taken about 1910 shows the boys in knickers and caps, the style for this period. Before the use of the present site in Memorial Park, many of the township's Fourth of July celebrations took place behind this clubhouse (see p. 110).

The Maplewood Club, sometimes called the Little Club, is located at 489 Ridgewood Road. It was founded in 1916 and offers tennis and bowling in addition to social functions. A touring car is coasting down the hill with tennis players in the background.

The local theater group, The Strollers, is one of the oldest continuously operating community theater groups in the country. In the photograph, Janet Rice, Peggy Stone, Bob Ostrander, and Bob Snyder are rehearsing at the Maplewood Woman's Club in 1950. They're rehearsing for the 58th production, *The Little Foxes*, by Lillian Hellman. The production director for the show was Mildred Memory, the founder of The Strollers in 1932. (Today's productions are staged at the Burgdorff Cultural Center.)

Borden Park, named after Milo Borden, the mayor during the 1930s, was cleaned up and improved in 1990. At the rededication ceremonies were, from left to right, Essex County Executive Nick D'Amato, Director of Community Development Rosemary Senatore Ciccone, Mayor Robert H. Grasmere, and U.S. Congressman Dean Gallo.

Memorial Park was created from remaining open land between Baker Street and Oakland Road and from the railroad to Valley Street. A row of houses on Baker Street and a store/apartment building on Dunnell Road were removed during the 1920s to complete this restful oasis.

A postcard labeled, "Rahway River, Maplewood, N.J.," was mailed to a friend at Williamsport, Pennsylvania, in 1906. The sender, Ruth, is bragging, "Isn't this a pretty spot?" It still is!

126

Set in a landscaped, 8-acre tract of land acquired from property of the Ward Homestead, the Community Swimming Pool was opened in August 1966. Members must be Maplewood residents and pay an annual fee. As shown here, it really is four pools: diving, main, training, and wading.

This image shows a sunny day at the Community Swimming Pool. In the forefront is a man and three children, a typical group enjoying this beautiful, award-winning facility.

Muskets are being fired in back of the Durand-Hedden House by Captain Littell's Company B of the New Jersey Militia. The reenactment of a military drill is an annual event during Muster Day, which is held in May.